Technology All Around Us

Computers

Anne Rooney

A⁺
Smart Apple Media

First published in 2005 by Franklin Watts
96 Leonard Street, London EC2A 4XD

Franklin Watts Australia
Level 17/207 Kent Street, Sydney NSW 2000

Produced by Arcturus Publishing Ltd.
26/27 Bickels Yard, 151–153 Bermondsey Street, London SE1 3HA

Series concept: Alex Woolf, Editor: Alex Woolf, Designer: Simon
Borrough, Picture researcher: Glass Onion Pictures

Picture Credits:
Corbis: 24 (Reuters / Jeff Christensen).
Pictorial Press: 16.
Science and Society Picture Library: 5 (Science Museum).
Science Photo Library: front cover, 4 (Maximilian Stock Ltd), 7 (Sam Ogden), 8 (George Haling), 9 (Peter Menzel), 10 (Philippe Plailly / Eurelios), 11 (David Parker), 12 (Peter Menzel), 13 (Peter Menzel), 14 (Alfred Pasieka), 15 (Alexander Tsiaras), 17 (Robert Holmgren, Peter Arnold Inc.), 19 (Peter Menzel), 20 (Peter Menzel), 21 (Sandia National Laboratories), 22 (Philippe Psaila), 23 (Geoff Tompkinson), 24 (Cordelia Molloy), 25 (Ed Young), 26 (Philippe Plailly / Eurelios), 27 (James King-Holmes), 28 (Pascal Goetgheluck), 29 (James King-Holmes).
Topham Picturepoint: 6 (Image Works), 18.

Published in the United States by Smart Apple Media
2140 Howard Drive West, North Mankato, Minnesota 56003

Library of Congress Cataloging-in-Publication Data

Rooney, Anne.
Computers / by Anne Rooney.
p. cm. — (Technology all around us)
Includes bibliographical references and index.
ISBN 1-58340-750-2
1. Computers—Juvenile literature. I. Title. II. Series.

QA76.23.R66 2005
004—dc22   2005040493

9 8 7 6 5 4 3 2 1

Contents

Computers are everywhere—not just on our desks, but in our cars, our pockets, around our homes, and even in the toy box. They don't all have a screen, keyboard, and mouse—many are hidden inside other things.

What Computers are Good at

Computers are useful for storing data and working with large amounts of information very quickly. For example, a computer could easily put an entire phone directory in numerical order of the phone numbers, or in reverse order of the names. It could figure out the total cost of all the goods in a supermarket in a matter of seconds.

The computers in this room control all of the machines in a steel-rolling mill.

These jobs would take a long time to do without a computer. Computers keep things running smoothly. They can monitor the world around them and control other equipment without taking a break or getting distracted.

Exciting Jobs for Computers

Some tasks couldn't be done at all without computers. Computers create special effects in movies such as the *Lord of the Rings* films. Computers on spacecraft let us explore distant planets using camera-equipped robots.

Computers help scientists predict earthquakes, volcanic eruptions, and climate changes. They help run big businesses and even whole countries, and monitor life-support equipment in hospitals.

Chess Champions
It is May 11, 1997. World chess champion Gary Kasparov has been beaten at chess by an IBM computer program called *Deep Blue.* Kasparov has been called the best chess player in history, but the computer can analyze 200 million possible board positions per second and never gets worried, distracted, or tired.

Looking Back

Mechanical Computers

The first type of computer was a mechanical engine that did calculations by moving cogs and wheels. It was designed by Charles Babbage in 1836. He continued improving his plans but never actually built his "analytical engine."

A working model of Babbage's machine has now been built in the Science Museum in London. It can perform calculations following coded instructions punched on cards. Babbage even designed a printer to go with his machine.

Part of the analytical engine designed by Charles Babbage. It was being built when he died but was never finished.

Personal Computers

Today, many people take personal computers for granted. Just 50 years ago, computers were so large and expensive that only large organizations could afford them.

Hardware and Software

The computer you use at home or at school probably has a screen, keyboard, mouse, and a box that contains all of the other parts, such as disk drives and electronic circuitry. All of this is called hardware.

Your computer also has software, or "programs." These are instructions that tell it how to function.

The Altair 8800 was one of the earliest personal computers.

Looking Forward

In Your Eye!
A company in the United States is developing special glasses that use a laser to draw an image directly on the back of the inside of the eyeball. People can still see the real world while wearing the glasses, but the screen image is shown on top.

Developers have found that in some cases blind people can see the images—so a computer can "see" for them and show them the surrounding world.

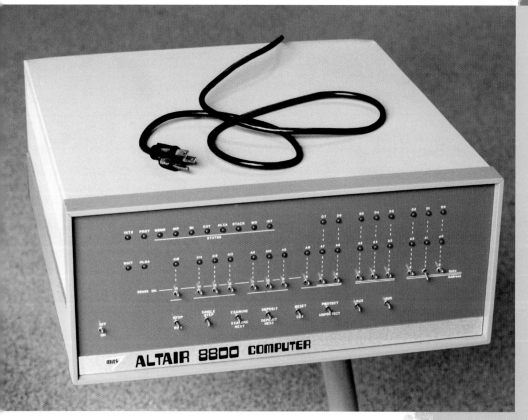

Looking Back

The First Personal Computer
The first computer that average people could buy was the Altair, launched in 1975. It was sold as a kit and had no keyboard, screen, disk drives, or software. Using little switches, people had to input a program each time they turned the computer on. The result of the program was displayed by lights to represent numbers.

Storage

Computers have many ways of storing data. You probably save your work on a hard or floppy disk. Other ways of storing information are on CD-ROM, DVD, or on a small memory card that you can plug into the computer.

Input and Output

All computers have a way to enter information (input) and a way to display that information and give answers (output).

For input, we use a keyboard, mouse, or touch screen. Some computers have special "tablets" that you write on with a plastic stylus, similar to a pen. Others have a scanner or barcode reader, and still others can understand speech.

For output, many computers use the screen and a printer, but some can talk, move things around, or control other equipment.

Many people now use small handheld computers called PDAs.

Many things around your house and school contain computers, even though they don't look like the computers you use for schoolwork and games.

Your washing machine or car might use computers. You can't use these to browse the Internet or write a letter—they can only do a very particular job. When a computer is built into something else and carries out a single task, it is called an embedded computer.

Cars of the future will use more computerized parts. This car has a computer that displays information about journey time, fuel consumption, and even the music playing on the CD.

Computerized Cars

Modern cars use embedded computers to control the engine settings. Their sensors relay what is going on and can change the settings quickly when needed.

If your car thinks it's too hot, it will change the mix of fuel and air and the speed at which the engine runs. Using computers like this means the car can adjust itself to use fuel economically, give a comfortable ride, and perform as well as possible.

Apollo's Guidance System

The first embedded computer was designed for the Apollo space missions in the 1960s. Each Apollo flight to the moon had two Apollo Guidance Computers. These computers handled navigation and controlled the movement of the main command module and the lunar lander (the part that landed on the moon).

The computers worked on their own, taking readings from the spacecraft without needing to contact mission control on Earth.

Many toys, like this doll, have computerized parts inside that respond to touch, sound, and movement.

Computers in the Kitchen

Lots of equipment around your kitchen probably uses computer technology to help you control it. Dishwashers, microwave ovens, refrigerators, and even toasters often have embedded computers. These computers follow a very simple set of instructions.

Looking Forward

Smart Toys

Lots of toys use computer chips. There is even a doll that complains if you dress it in an evening dress in the morning!

Soon, some toys will learn what you like and don't like, develop their own personalities, and respond to you like a real friend or pet. Many will react to what's happening on a TV program or DVD. You may even be able to tell your toys what to do using a mobile phone or the Internet.

Computers don't always work by themselves. The Internet links computers around the world so that they can share files and information. It uses the wires, cables, and radio signals of the phone network to transfer information.

In a cybercafe, people can use computers connected to the World Wide Web while enjoying a drink and a snack.

Networking the World

The Internet developed from a network called the ARPANET, which linked four universities together in 1969. It was used for e-mail, for transferring and sharing computer files, and for early computer games. The network quickly spread around the U.S. and to other countries. It became known as the Internet in 1983.

The World Wide Web

The World Wide Web was invented in 1990. At first, the pages could only show words or pictures, not a combination of the two. The first web browser that could show both appeared in 1993.

Now, web pages feature sound, movies, and animations as well as pictures and words.

Fast Internet search engines mean that computer users can find information on any topic in seconds. Users can shop, watch what is happening in distant places, play games, listen to the radio, watch TV or special "Webcasts," and download free software.

Looking Forward

Online Medicine

Scientists are working on pacemakers and other implanted medical aids that will check the patient's condition and send regular updates to doctors via the Internet. In an emergency, the equipment will send a call for help.

Patients will therefore need to make fewer trips to the hospital for checkups, and will feel confident that their doctors are monitoring their condition.

Technology in Action

SETI

Most computers are idle much of the time. In 1994, two scientists working at the SETI (Search for Extraterrestrial Intelligence) Institute decided that idle computers could do useful work for their project. SETI looks at data from radio telescopes, searching for patterns that could be a message from other life in space.

The result was SETI@home, a free screen saver that runs when a computer isn't doing anything else, examining chunks of the telescope data and sending the results back to SETI.

The SETI@home screen saver shows what it is doing as it searches for patterns in radio telescope data.

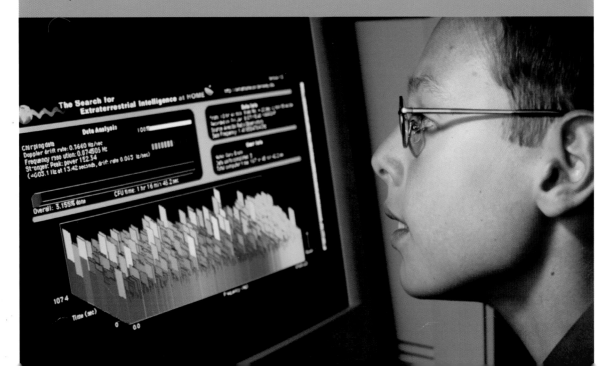

You've probably played quite a few computer games. They range from quick games you can play on a Web site to long, complicated games that let you build and manage an empire, rock band, or football team.

Working Hard to Play Hard

Playing games is very hard work for computers! Because most games have lots of detailed graphics (pictures) that move quickly, the computer has to work hard to keep up. It needs to follow the instructions of the game and the moves you choose, and it needs to send information to the screen to constantly redraw the picture.

In fact, the trend for faster and faster games with more pictures has helped to drive computer development forward quickly.

Looking Back

Pong

The first computer game was called Pong. It was similar to ping-pong. Players bounced a white spot back and forth on a screen using two paddles. It was very simple. The picture was black and white, and the paddles were moved by keys on the keyboard.

You can play with a pong emulator (a copy) on the Web. Use a search engine such as Google to look for "pong emulator."

These two boys are playing against each other in a boxing video game.

The virtual reality landscape shown on the screens changes as the man walks across the sensitive tread on the floor.

Virtual Reality

The next generation of computer games is likely to use virtual reality (VR). This means creating an imaginary world that you can move around in while you play. Some virtual reality exists already. VR goggles show you what is happening in an imaginary, three-dimensional world, and a virtual reality glove allows you to feel things. VR isn't used only for games—it can be used to train people for tasks such as performing surgery or flying planes.

 Looking Forward

VR Suits

People who write computer games are very excited by VR. One day, people may be able to put on an entire VR suit and use their own actions to produce movements in the virtual world of the game. They will be able to feel the game environment, as well as see and hear it. Imagine being able to feel the thrust of piloting a space vehicle or feel cold while exploring a polar ice cap.

Computers can make images of places that people cannot experience or view in any other way. Using computers, people can see pictures of outer space, the inside of the human body, and the bottom of the sea.

Seeing Without Light

The human eye can show an image only if there is enough light. But by using a computer, people can collect information using infrared, ultrasound, X-ray, and radio signals. This information can then be shown as a picture, a technique known as imaging.

For example, an infrared picture shows a heat map. An infrared picture taken from the air can show living beings in a landscape, even in the dark.

Technology in Action

An infrared photo of a house. A computer has been used to change measurements from an infrared sensor into a heat map of the house. The parts that lose the most heat (windows and roof) are yellow or white.

Back from the Dead
It is 1998, and scientists are using computers to reconstruct the face of a man who died 5,300 years ago. The man's mummified body had been preserved in ice in Italy.

First, scientists work from scans of the head to create a model of the skull. A laser scans the model, and then a computer figures out what the face looked like when the ice man was alive. Finally, the computer is connected to equipment that cuts a plastic model of the man's head.

Making Faces

A computer can take information from a skull and combine it with information about human faces to show what a person looked like when he or she was alive. This is called visualization. It has been done to create pictures of long-dead Egyptian pharaohs from their mummified bodies, and to make images of murder victims.

Computers can also "age" pictures of people who have been lost to help police try to trace and identify them years later.

Looking Back

Photofit and E-fit

Years ago, police asked crime witnesses to help them build a picture of a criminal by putting together photos of parts of a face. They used pictures of eyes, noses, mouths, eyebrows, ears, and hair to construct a face.

Now, a more advanced system called e-fit is used. This uses computer images and lets people make more changes to the image, adjusting the skin tone and hair, for instance.

From X rays and scans of her mummified body, computer images show what this ancient Egyptian woman, named Ta·bes, looked like when she was alive.

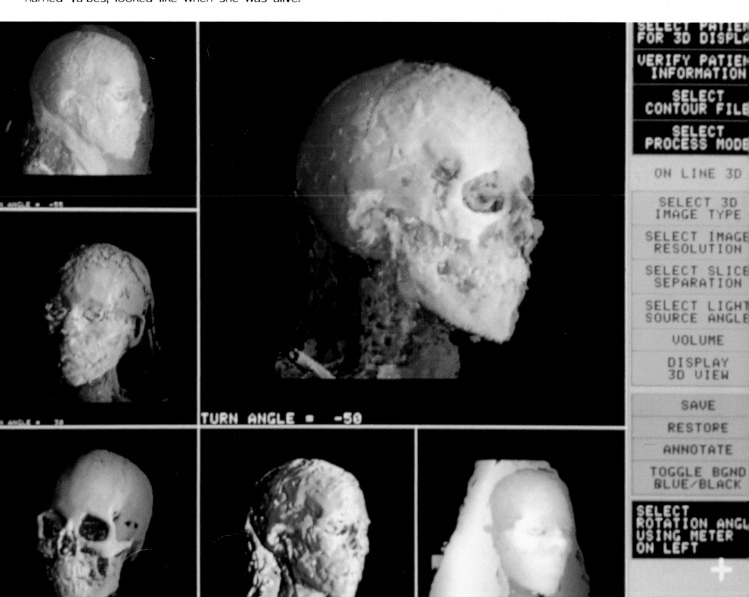

Many modern movies use special effects created with the help of computers. Some movies are created completely on computer and use real actors only for the voices.

Adding Virtual Characters

In films such as the *Lord of the Rings* trilogy and the *Harry Potter* series, real people seem to act alongside imaginary creatures. These creatures are created entirely on computer. The actors behave as though the creatures are present, but, in fact, there is nothing there. They are all added by computer later.

When there are lots of similar characters—such as the army of orcs in the *Lord of the Rings* movies—each "character" is programmed to act individually. One character might yell if attacked, while a different one might gasp. When all of these are put together in a battle or crowd scene, the variety makes the action look realistic.

The character of Gollum in the *Lord of the Rings* movies was created completely on computers.

Technology in Action

Blue Screen

Before computer animation was used to add fantasy such as monsters or people flying, a method called "blue screen" was used. To make an actor fly, for instance, he or she was filmed acting in front of a completely blue background. A filter was then used to cut the blue out of the film, and the background sky or landscape was added in behind the actor.

Making Movies

Movies such as *Shrek* and *Finding Nemo* are made completely on computer. The characters are designed in different stages—their shape, their surfaces (skin, hair, or fur), and their movements.

The computer is then told the action of a scene, and it moves the characters around. The computer has a complete three-dimensional model of the action, so the director can move the viewpoint around.

Finding Nemo

Pixar Studios needed two and a half years to make the computer-animated movie *Finding Nemo*. The animators began by studying real fish and learning about their movements. They then converted these to software instructions for the fish they had designed.

At first, the fish were drawn as wire-frame models. These showed just the structure of the body and were used to program movements. A particular challenge for the animators was copying the play of light on water as seen from beneath the surface.

To help animators show movement realistically, sensors attached to an actor's body capture his movements. The information is stored on computer and used to help design the movement of animated characters.

17

Artificial intelligence (AI) is the name given to computers that can think for themselves. No one has yet made a truly intelligent machine—but many people are trying.

Are Intelligent Machines Possible?

An intelligent machine would be able to figure out how to do things for which it didn't have full instructions. It would need to be able to learn and to make judgments. It is difficult to say exactly what an intelligent machine would be like, because people don't agree on what intelligence really is.

Expert Systems

Although we don't have AI, we do have expert systems. These are computers that have been given a great deal of information about a complicated subject, such as law or medicine. An expert system can quickly make expert decisions by comparing new information with all of the information it has already.

An expert system makes decisions much faster than a person and doesn't forget any details. But it can only work with the information it's been given. A human doctor makes judgments about a patient while listening to him or her describe what is wrong. A computer can't pick up clues from body language or use intuition.

In the film *Artificial Intelligence*, people and AI robots are hard to tell apart.

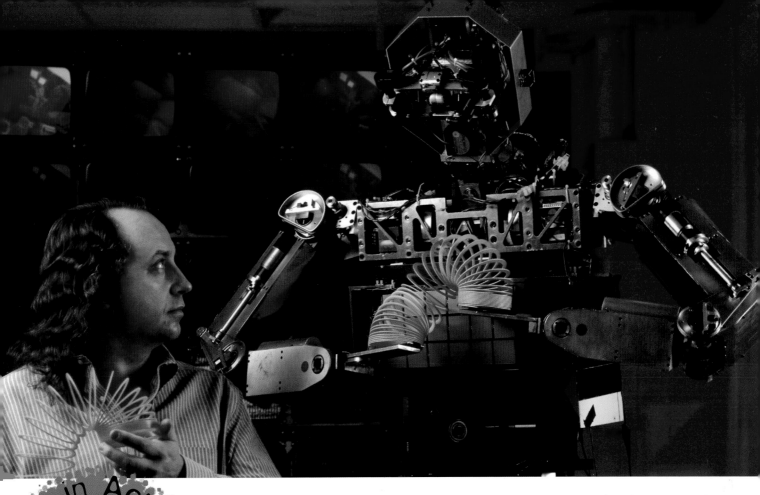

This robot is part of an experiment in artificial intelligence. It is learning how to play with a Slinky toy, adjusting its own programming as it finds out about the toy.

The Loebner Prize

In 1990, Hugh Loebner began a competition for people to invent an intelligent machine. The prize is $100,000, and the competition is still running. There is a prize of $2,000 each year for the best attempt.

To win, a computer has to convince a person that he or she is talking to another person and not a machine. In their attempts to win the prize, many people have developed "chatterbots," computers that can chat with people.

Looking Back

Eliza

In 1966, Joseph Weizenbaum wrote a computer program that he called Eliza. It wasn't an AI system, but it acted somewhat like a person, holding a conversation in text on the screen. Many people thought it really was intelligent, and they enjoyed talking to it!

Eliza worked by recognizing some of the words that the person typed and then using the words to make up questions. It was programmed to work with the rules of English grammar, but it did not really understand language.

Technology in Action

Robots are machines controlled by computers. The computer may be built into the robot, or it might be separate and connected to it. The robots we see in science fiction movies are quickly becoming real. Most of them don't look at all like people, as they do in films, but that could change.

This robot follows carefully written instructions that enable it to juggle.

What Makes a Robot?

Most robots have sensors that tell them about conditions around them. For instance, they might be able to tell the temperature, to figure out where things are, or to gauge sunlight. Information from the sensors is used, along with computer instructions, to tell the robot what to do. Robots can also be given instructions directly by people.

Looking Back

Automated Factories

Today, everything from computers to chocolate is made in largely automated factories. This process began in the 1970s, when the first factories began using robots. Car factories used robots for tasks such as cutting and shaping metal body panels, spray painting cars, and assembling the parts.

It didn't always work smoothly. In 1985, an automated factory opened by General Motors malfunctioned, with robots adding the wrong parts to cars, and spray paint robots spraying each other.

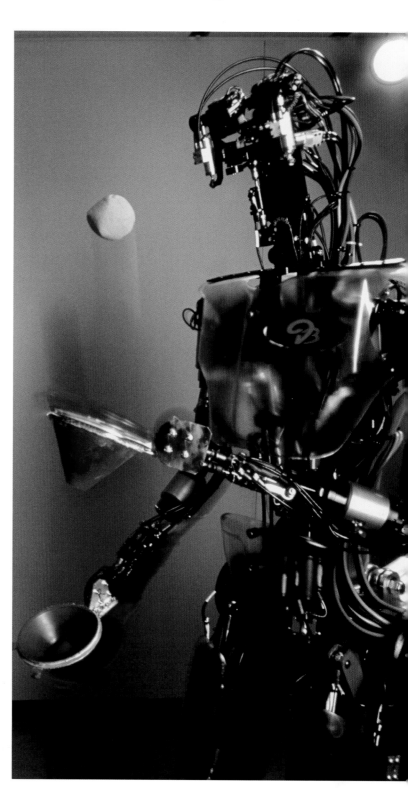

Tasks for Robots

Robots excel at jobs that require precise control, such as building tiny computer circuits. They can also be sent into places that would be dangerous for people. Remote controlled robots are sometimes used to explore volcanoes or "sniff" for explosives.

Looking Forward

Snow Rescue

American Rush Robinett developed a set, or "swarm," of small robots to help find skiers or hikers lost under snow following an avalanche.

The robots in the swarm communicate with each other, sharing information about their location and any people they find. Sharing information means they can reach a buried skier much more quickly than a human search team or a single robot searcher.

Getting Better

The first robots simply followed detailed instructions. The newest robots use systems called neural networks. These copy the way the human brain works, enabling the robot to learn. Already, a robot can learn to find its way around a room and "remember" something it has tried before to help it make decisions in the future.

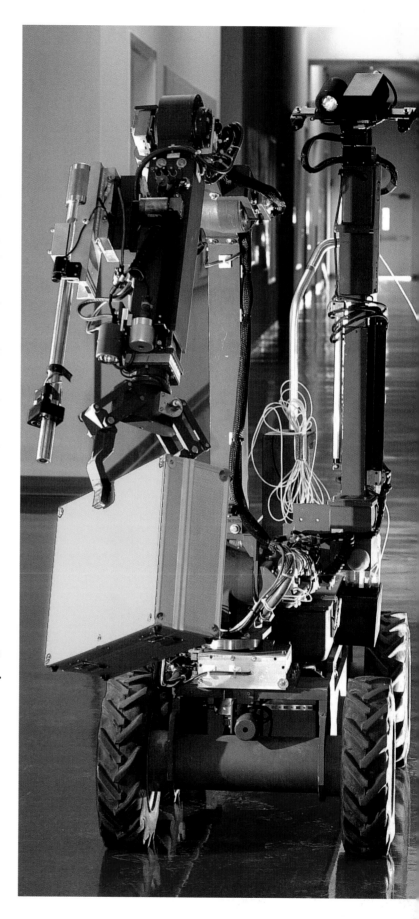

A Wolverine bomb disposal robot carries a suitcase bomb, keeping real police and bomb disposal experts safe from a dangerous task.

Computers are used in many areas of modern warfare. They help to fly planes, pilot ships and tanks, guide missiles and bombs to their targets, and protect soldiers in the battlefield.

A French soldier uses an infrared sensor that enables him to detect the body heat of people hidden in the grass and bushes.

Technology in Action

Clothes that Can Hear

Dana Reynolds, a weaver, is working on a new type of combat suit for soldiers. Her cloth has two layers of wires and one of cotton, woven together. The wires and microphones hidden in the suit's buttons pick up sounds made by an approaching enemy before the soldier can hear them.

A computer figures out where the sounds are coming from and sends the information to a laptop or PDA (a small, handheld computer) the soldier carries. The cloth can also be used for parachutes and tents.

Vehicles with No Crew

Some of the newest planes and tanks can go into battle completely on their own—without a human crew. Planes without human pilots are known as unmanned air vehicles (UAVs). Using the latest computer technology, they can navigate to the target or battle area.

Smart Bombs

Bombs and missiles often have embedded computers to help them find their targets. They use radio and satellite signals to navigate and can take readings from the ground they are flying over. They can also adjust their path if the target moves.

War Games

Computer programs help train soldiers and marines to deploy troops and weapons. Using programs similar to war games, they learn how and when to move troops into position, and what the best tactics are for different situations on the battlefield.

The program shows what is likely to happen following the decisions soldiers make. It is a useful preparation for real-life battle.

Looking Back

Code-Breaking at Bletchley Park
During World War II, all armies sent coded messages to control their troops. The Germans had a special coding machine. It made up a very complicated code that changed each day.

A team of mathematicians at Bletchley Park, England, built the first modern computer, called Colossus, in order to break the code. They were then able to figure out the meaning of the secret German messages.

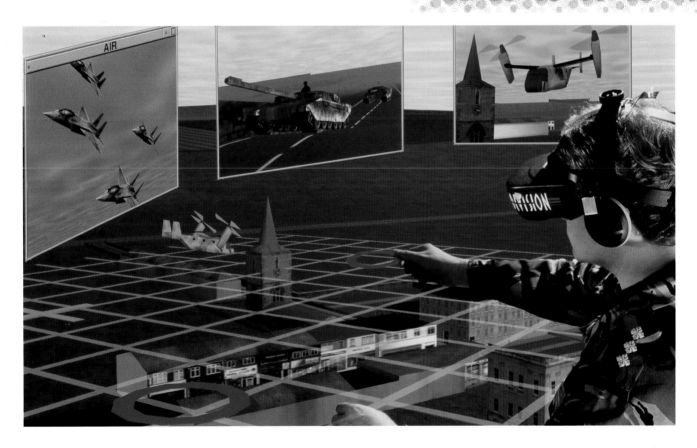

A soldier using a virtual reality system in training. He places circles to show where to move tanks or aircraft on a map that is made by computer from maps of a real place.

Modern criminals use computers not only to plan attacks but also to carry them out.

A group of computer hackers at a conference in New York, 2002. Computer security experts sometimes ask hackers to break into their systems to help them find and improve weaknesses.

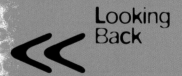

Crime on Computer

Computer crime comes in many forms. Some criminals hack into computer systems to destroy, change, or steal valuable information.

Spies might steal secret information about national security, political plans, or business developments. Some thieves use computers to break into bank accounts or steal credit card details so that they can take money from people.

Writing and distributing viruses is another type of computer crime. A virus is a destructive program that spreads from one computer to another. It can destroy saved data or disrupt people's use of the computer. Virus damage is very costly to repair.

Looking Back

Phone Phreaking

In the early 1970s, before computers were commonplace, "phone phreakers" hacked into phone networks to get free phone calls. They used a whistle and a "blue box" that turned sounds into tones that the phone routers understood.

One of the first phone phreakers used the name Cap'n Crunch because the whistle he used came free in a box of Cap'n Crunch breakfast cereal. Many pioneers of the home computer industry began as phone phreakers.

"I Love You" Virus

It is 2000, and a computer virus known as the Lovebug or "I love you" virus has spread around the world. It has cost businesses an estimated $7 billion in lost work time and effort spent cleaning infected computers.

The virus spreads as an e-mail attachment—a file sent along with an e-mail message. The man who wrote the virus, Onel De Guzman, remains free. He lives in the Philippines, where there is no law against writing and releasing a computer virus.

Cyberterrorism

Cyberterrorism is terrorism carried out using computers instead of bombs and guns. A cyberterrorist could break into an air traffic control computer system, for instance, and give false information to pilots so that their planes crash.

Some cyberterrorist attacks might not kill anyone, but they could cost governments or businesses billions of dollars. If terrorists disabled the computers in the stock exchange or in major banks, trade and industry would be at a standstill until they were fixed.

Air traffic controllers depend on computers to show them where planes are in the sky. An attack on this system could cause a fatal plane crash.

A computer model of the inside of the Basilica of St. Francis in Assisi, Italy. "Virtual tourists" can now experience places without visiting them.

Computers are often used to create models, or copies, of a real object or situation. A computer model of a plane, for example, would be used to test the design, making sure it was stable in bad weather.

A situation such as a terrorist attack on a big city can be modeled to test different responses to it.

Making Models

People use computers to model things that would be expensive or dangerous to test in the real world. Architects make computer models of new bridges and buildings to see what will happen in a high wind, lots of traffic, or even in an earthquake.

People who are learning to pilot planes or ships begin by using a computer program that acts like a real plane or ship. If they make mistakes, no one will be hurt, and it will not cost anything. A model like this is called a simulation.

Looking Forward

Living on Venus
Scientists are considering the possibility of changing the planet Venus so that people can live there.

Long before we have the technology to make any real changes, scientists are working with computer models to explore how we might use chemical reactions to change the atmosphere, and how much energy and other resources would be needed. The models show what will happen over time, helping to prevent an unforeseen disaster.

Predicting the Future

People also use models to show what will happen over time and to make predictions. Weather forecasts are a type of model; they use information about past weather patterns and current conditions to predict what will happen next.

Volcano!

It is 2004, and scientists in Italy are using complicated computer models to help them plan an evacuation. They are worried that the volcano Vesuvius, which destroyed the Roman towns of Pompeii and Herculaneum in 79 B.C., will soon erupt again. The volcano is very close to the modern city of Naples.

The computer models show scientists how quickly the lava will flow, how far and how fast super-heated air from the volcano will travel, and how quickly people will be able to move out of the city using roads and railways.

A pilot uses a simulator to learn to land safely at Heathrow Airport, London, England.

Most people think nothing of using a mouse, keyboard, and screen. But for some people with disabilities, computers mean much more. The computers might have special input and output devices to help people use them. Computers can give some people freedoms they could not otherwise enjoy.

A camera tracks this man's eye movements to move a pointer on the computer screen, allowing him to control items in his home.

Special Computers

People who cannot use their hands to work with a computer have many other options. Since the 1980s, there have been systems that allow people to use their feet or even their mouth to work with a computer. Now, there are devices that allow whole-body movements or large gestures to control a computer.

Some computers can even respond to the movement of a person's eye, so that just reading across and down a screen is enough to move the picture onto the next line of text. Or a person can "type" simply by focusing on letters on an on-screen keyboard.

Home Help

Computerized equipment in the home or workplace can help people with restricted mobility and other disabilities. Houses can be completely linked by computer so that everything from controlling the heating to opening the windows and curtains can be handled using a single remote control panel. This can be voice-activated if necessary.

Technology in Action

Stephen Hawking

Stephen Hawking is a brilliant physicist who is completely disabled by a disease that affects his nerves and muscles. He uses a specially built wheelchair and computer.

His computer produces a voice for him. He cannot speak, but uses a handheld switch to tell the computer what he wants to say. The computer then "says" it for him using a special voice synthesizer, or saves it for later if it is work for a book or article. Hawking can manage about 15 words a minute.

Looking Forward

A Helping Hand—or Foot

Medical scientists are looking at ways of linking artificial limbs into a person's nervous system. This would mean that an artificial arm or leg could be moved in the same way as a real one—the person would need only desire to move it.

The electrical impulses from the person's nerves would feed into electrical circuits controlling the artificial limb. Computer technology would convert the impulses from the nerves into instructions to move the new limb.

This robotic hand is controlled by electrical nerve impulses picked up by sensors on the man's forearm. It moves in the same way as his own hand.

Timeline

1836 Charles Babbage designs his first analytical engine, a mechanical computer.

1840–46 Ada Lovelace, daughter of poet Lord Byron, works with Babbage to write the first computer programs for his analytical engine.

1944 Colossus, the first electronic computer, is used at Bletchley Park, England, to decode secret German messages in World War II.

1950 English mathematician Alan Turing suggests it might be possible to create a machine that can think—the basis of AI.

1952 IBM makes the first mass-produced computer.

1969 ARPANET, the forerunner of the Internet, links the computers of four U.S. universities.

1975 The Altair is sold as a kit to build at home, sparking the home computer revolution.

1976 The first Apple computer, the Apple I, goes on sale as a kit. It is replaced the same year by the Apple II.

1982 The invention of the three-inch floppy disk. Before this, disks were first eight inches and then five inches across.

1983 ARPANET becomes the Internet.

1983 The Apple Lisa is the first personal computer to use a mouse, windows, icons, and menus instead of typed instructions.

1985 The first version of Microsoft Windows is released.

1990 The invention of the World Wide Web.

1993 The development of the first Web browser that can show pages that mix words and pictures.

1996 The first successful PDA, the PalmPilot, goes on sale. Other groups had worked on similar products since 1986, but this was the first to be successful.

2002 The "tablet PC" is the first computer with as much power as an ordinary desktop or laptop computer that uses a stylus for handwriting and sketching as its main input method.

Glossary

artificial intelligence A computer system or machine that can think and learn for itself.

deploying Spreading out and positioning.

embedded computer A computer system inside another piece of equipment that carries out a specific task.

hack Break into a computer system without permission, getting around security systems and passwords.

hardware Pieces of equipment that make up a computer.

implanted Fitted inside.

impulses Tiny bursts or pulses of electricity that carry a message.

infrared An invisible wavelength of electromagnetic radiation that comes below red light in the spectrum.

intuition An insight or sense of something that comes without thinking or reasoning.

laptop A portable computer.

laser An intense beam of light that can be used for cutting or measuring objects.

life-support equipment Hospital equipment used to keep someone alive. It often involves controlling the heartbeat and breathing.

monitor Keep track of by taking regular readings or making regular checks.

neural network A computer system that copies the way the human brain works.

pacemaker A piece of equipment put into the heart in an operation to keep the heartbeat regular.

PDA A small, handheld computer.

phone router Equipment for sending phone calls along the right wires and cables to make the connection needed for one phone to contact another.

program A set of computer instructions.

screen saver A still or moving picture shown on a computer screen when the computer is not being used for other work.

sensor Equipment that takes readings or measurements from the environment.

software One or more computer programs, or sets of instructions.

tablet A computer or attachment for a computer on which people write or draw using a plastic stick called a stylus.

ultrasound Sound waves above the pitch of those that can be heard by people, used to gain information to make images of things inside or beneath surfaces we can't see through.

virtual reality An environment that exists only in a model created by a computer, but that seems real when experienced with suitable equipment.

voice synthesizer An electronic device used to create human speech using a computer.

Web browser A computer program for looking at and moving between Web pages.

Further Information

Further Reading

Coleman, Michael. *Crashing Computers*. New York: Scholastic, 1999.

Kerrod, Robin, and Sharon Ann Holgate. *The Way Science Works*. New York: Dorling Kindersley, 2002.

Rooney, Anne. *Internet Technologies*. North Mankato, Minn.: Chrysalis, 2003.

Woolf, Alex. *21st Century Debates: Artificial Intelligence*. North Mankato, Minn.: Chrysalis, 2003.

Web sites

http://www.maxmon.com/history.htm
A history of computing and calculating technologies from the earliest times to the present.

http://www.computerhistory.org/exhibits/online_exhibitions.html
On-line exhibitions and information from the Computer History Museum in California.

http://whyfiles.org
Current science news, including computer news, in an easy-to-understand form. The archives have many fascinating computer-related stories.